200 Omelettes
Egg Di[shes]

Charles Herman Senn

Copyright © 2015
All rights reserved.
ISBN: 1539551067
ISBN-13: 978-1539551065

CONTENTS

OMELETTES. 9
HOW TO MAKE AN OMELET. 9
   Kidneys and Tomatoes. 11
   Omelette Naturelle (Plain Omelet). 11
   Omelette a l'Anglaise (English Omelet)................................11
   Omelette aux Fines Herbes {Savoury Omelet).....................11
   Omelette aux Asperger (Asparagus Omelet). 12
   Omelette a la Bonne femine. 12
   Omelette a la Charentiere. 13
   Omelette a la Bernoise. 13
   Omelette a la Raphael 13
   Omelette aux Polreaux (Leek Omelet). 14
   Petites Omelettes a la Marechale. 14
   Omelettes gratinees au Parmesan (Parmesan Omelet). 15
   Omelettes Duchesse a I'Ecarlate (Small Omelets stuffed with Tongue)..15
   Omelette aux Huitres (Oyster Omelet). 16
   Omelette a la Gordon. 16
   Omelette Savoyarde. 17
   Omelet au Jambon (Ham Omelet). 17
   Omelette aux Anchois (Anchovy Omelet). 17
   Omelette aux Sardines (Sardine Omelet). 17
   Omelette a l'Indienne (Curry Omelet)...................................17
   Omelette au Homard (Lobster Omelet). 18
   Omelette aux Oignons (Onion Omelet). 18
   Omelette a la Bearnaise. 18
   Omelette a la Bayonne. 18
   Omelette a la Cervelle (Brain Omelet). 18
   Omelette aux Champignons (Mushroom Omelet)................19
   Omelette aux Concombres (Cucumher Omelet)...................19
   Omelette aux Epinards (Spinach Omelet). 19
   Omelette au Fromage (Cheese Omelet)................................19
   Omelette au Lentilles (Lentil Omelet). 19
   Omelette aux Rognons (Kidney Omelet). 20
   Omelette aux Tomates (Tomato Omelet). 20
   Omelette aux Truffles (Truffle Omelet). 20

- Omelette Soufflees au Poisson (Fish Puff Omelet). 20
- Omelette Souffle aux fines herbes (Savoury Puff Omelet). ..21

PLATS D'OEUFS— EGG DISHES. 21
- Oeufs poches au Vin blanc (Poached Eggs in White Wine). 21
- Oeufs aux Nouilles a la Carola. 22
- Oeufs a la Suzette. 22
- Oeufs a la Princesse (Egg Darioles). 22
- Fricassee d'Oeufs (Fricasseed Eggs). 23
- Oeufs a la Dreux. 24
- Oeufs a la Milanaise. 24
- Oeufs a la Boston. 25
- Oeufs brouilles (Scrambled Eggs). 26
- Oeufs brouilles aux Pointes d'Asperges. 26
- Oeufs brouilles aux Anchois (Anchovy Buttered Eggs)........27
- Oeufs brouilles aux Trufles (Scrambled Eggs with Truffles). 27
- Oeufs brouilles a la Turque (Eggs, Turkish Style). 28
- Oeufs garnis a la Coquette. 28
- Oeufs Miroire a la Princesse. 29
- Oeufs farcis aux Crevettes (Stuffed Eggs with Prawns)........30
- Oeufs a la Carnot. 30
- Croquettes aux Oeufs (Egg Croquettes). 31
- Cromesquis aux Oeufs (Kromeskies of Eggs). 31
- Oeufs en Chaud-froid. 32
- Oeufs a la Colbert. 32
- Oeufs frits au Beurre noir (Fried Eggs in Brown Butter). 33
- Oeufs a la Parmentier..33
- Oeufs a l'Ecarlate (Poached Eggs with Tongue)...................34
- Oeufs a la Courbet (Cold). 34
- Oeufs frits a la Fermiere. 34
- Oeufs poches a la Tomate (Poached Eggs, Tomato Sauce)...35
- Oeufs en Matelote (Eggs, Seaman's Way). 35
- Pyramide d'Oeufs a la Reforme. 35
- Oeufs a la Garfield..36
- Oeufs a la Messina..36
- Oeufs a la Carigen. 36
- Oeufs a la Gagnor (Cold)..36
- Oeufs poches a la Reine (Poached Eggs, Queen's Style).......37
- Oeufs St. Jacques (Eggs, St. James's Style)..........................37

Oeufs a la Medicis. 37
Oeufs a l'Indienne (Curried Eggs). 38
Oeufs en Feuilletage (Eggs in Puff-pastry). 38
Oeufs a la Tripe. 39
Oeufs mollets a la Bechamel. 39
Oeufs au Beurre Noisette. 39
Oeufs a la Waldimir. 40
Cotelettes aux Oeufs (Egg Cutlets). 40
Ragout d'Oeufs a la Francaise. 40
Oeufs en Cocottes. 40
Oeufs brouilles a l'Italienne (Italian Scrambled Eggs)..........41
Oeufs brouilles an Jambon. 41
Oeufs a la Creole. 41
Oeufs a la Mode de Caen. 41
Oeufs a la Carmelite. 41
Oeufs a la Chipolata, ...42
Oeufs a la Comtesse..42
Oeufs a la Creme de Volaille. 42
Oeufs a la Coque en Surprise (Cold). 42
Oeufs a la Pache...42
Oeufs a la Pasqual (Cold). 43
Oeufs poches a l'Imperiale (Cold)...43

ABBREVIATED RECIPES FOR OTHER EGG DISHES.......43
Oeufs a l'Americaine. 43
Oeufs a l'Ancienne. 43
Oeufs a l'Andalouse (Cold). 44
Oeufs a l'Arlequin. 44
Oeufs a l'Aumale. 44
Oeufs a l'Aurore. 44
Oeufs a la Bearnaise. 44
Oeufs a la Bedford. 44
Oeufs a la Belle-Helene. 44
Oeufs a la Benedictine. 45
Oeufs a la Bercy..45
Oeufs a la Bohemienne. 45
Oeufs a la Bouchere. 45
Oeufs a la Bourguignonne. 45
Oeufs a la Brebant. 45
Oeufs a la Bresilienne. 45

Oeufs a la Bretonne. 46
Oeufs a la Bruxelloise. 46
Oeufs a la Careme. 46
Oeufs a la Cardinal. 46
Oeufs a la Chantilly. 46
Oeufs a la Chasseur. 46
Oeufs a la Chivry. 47
Oeufs a la Clamart. 47
Oeufs a la Cluny. 47
Oeufs a la Colombine. 47
Oeufs a la Conde. 47
Oeufs a la Crecy. 47
Oeufs a la Czarina (Cold). 47
Oeufs a la Diable. 48
Oeufs a la Duchesse. 48
Oeufs a la Elisabeth. 48
Oeufs a l'Espagnole. 48
Oeufs a la Florentine. 48
Oeufs a la Forestiere. 48
Oeufs a la Gambetta. 48
Oeufs a la Hongroise. 49
Oeufs a la Hussarde. 49
Oeufs a la Khedive. 49
Oeufs a la Lorette. 49
Oeufs a la Lucullus. 49
Oeufs a la Mireille. 49
Oeufs a la Monaco. 50
Oeufs a la Mornay. 50
Oeufs a la Mosaique (Cold). 50
Oeufs a la Nantua. 50
Oeufs a la Niqoise. 50
Oeufs a l'Orleans. 50
Oeufs a la Palestine. 50
Oeufs a la Perigueux. 51
Oeufs a la Portugaise. 51
Oeufs a la Poulette. 51
Oeufs a la Princiere. 51
Oeufs a la Rachel. 51
Oeufs a la Reine Margot. 51

    Oeufs a la Romaine. 51
    Oeufs a la Rossini. 52
    Oeufs a la Sevigne. 52
    Oeufs a la Soubise. 52
    Oeufs a la Turbigo. 52
    Oeufs a la Vatel. 52
    Oeufs a la Verdi. 52
    Oeufs a la Victoria. 52
    Oeufs a la Yvette. 53
    Oeufs a la Zingara. 53
Miscellaneous 53
    Bouquet Garni 53
    Nouille Paste (Pate Nouilles). 53
    Salpicon. 54
    Sauce Allemande (German Sauce). 54
    Sauce Anchois (Anchovy Sauce). 55
    Sauce Aurora. 55
    Sauce Bechamel. 55
    Sauce Bordeaux. 56
    Sauce Bearnaise. 56
    Sauce Bordelaise (Claret Sauce). 57
    Brown Fish Sauce (Sauce Brune, Brown Sauce). 57
    Sauce Cardinal. 58
    Sauce Chaud-froid, blanche (White Chaud-froid Sauce). 58
    Sauce Colbert aux Fines Herbes (Brown Herb Sauce). 59
    Curry Sauce. (See "Sauce Indienne") 59
    Sauce Demi-Glace (Half-Glaze Sauce). 59
    Sauce Espagnole (Spanish Sauce). 60
    Sauce Homard (Lobster Sauce). 61
    Sauce Indienne (Indian Curry Sauce). 61
    Sauce Italienne (Italian Sauce). 62
    Sauce Madere (Madeira Sauce). 62
    Sauce Mornay. 62
    Sauce Mousseline Verte (Green Mousseline Sauce, cold). ... 63
    Melted Butter Sauce (Sauce Anglaise). 63
    Sauce Nantua. 64
    Onion Sauce (Sauce aux Oignons). 64
    Sauce Perigueux (Truffle Sauce, Perigord Sauce). 64
    Sauce Piquante (Sharp Sauce). 65

Sauce Poivrade (Pepper Satice). 65
Sauce Remoulade..66
Sauce Supreme...66
Sauce Tomate (Tomato Sauce). 67
Sauce Venitienne. 67
Sauce Veloutee (Velvet Sauce). 68
Simple White Sauce...68
Sauce Chivry...69
Sauce Choron. 69
Sauce a la Creme (Cream Sauce)..69
Sauce Paprika...69

OMELETTES.

That the nutritive properties of eggs are by far greater than that of almost any other food product is an acknowledged fact. It is also true that by the help of eggs we are enabled to prepare more appetizing, dainty, and wholesome dishes than we can with other materials that can be cooked on the "hasty principle." There are so many easy, inexpensive and palatable ways of preparing eggs for the table that it seems strange so many cooks should confine themselves to the alternative methods of boiling and frying them.

AN OMELET PAN

Omelets are no doubt the most popular form of dishes produced from eggs, although the making thereof is but seldom properly understood in this country; there is, as a rule, a certain knack, care, and delicacy needed in the manipulation in order to prepare a correct continental omelet. Those can easily be acquired and the best way is by means of practice.

HOW TO MAKE AN OMELET.

The best and most convenient way to make an omelet is to break six or eight eggs, according to the size required. It is unwise to attempt a lager sized omelet unless one is a master hand at it.

The eggs used must be fresh and must be well but over beaten, just long enough to thoroughly amalgamate the whites with the yolks.

A little cream or milk, say a tablespoonful of either to three eggs, added will make the omelet lighter and moister.

The pan used must be quite clean; it must only be used for omelets and must never be allowed to be washed. The best way to clean it is to make it hot over the fire and to rub the inside with a handful of coarse salt and then wipe it with a paper and rubber.

The butter, which must be fresh (not salt butter), is next put into the pan. About an ounce is the average quantity required for four eggs, the less used the better. It must be allowed to get quite hot but not burning. More the eggs are poured in.

Season the eggs with salt, pepper and in the case of savoury omelets with chopped herbs; avoid the use of pungent spices.

Cooking is the next important item. As soon as the eggs poured into the pan, shake it by its handle with one hand and with the other (the right hand) stir the contents of the pan, slowly ats first and quickly as the eggs begin to set,

The Fire must be bright, but not too fierce.

Shaping the omelet is the next operation. This is effected by tilting the pan a little, slipping a thin bladed knife under the edge, and so giving the omelet the shape of an oval cushion or plump half-moon shape. Allow it to form a crust i.e. to blown very slightly over the fine and turn immediately on a hot dish. An omelet should be sent to table immediately it is cooked, and should not on any account be allowed to stand, because it is apt to become tough.

Turning out an Omelet.

To do this correctly and successfully, hold the pan by its handle with the right hand, the palm of the hand being underneath the handle. Hold an oblong warm dish in the left hand, bring the outer edge of the pan close to the centre of the dish, turn out the omelet by turning the pan upside down, and then quickly remove the pan.

The process of making a simple omelet should not take more than five minutes.

Kidneys and Tomatoes.

Slice six sheep's kidneys, previously skinned, fry eight thinly-cut rashers of fat bacon, then fry the slices of kidney in the bacon fat. When slightly cooked, add three peeled and sliced tomatoes, season with salt and pepper, and cook all together—i.e. toss in the pan for another three minutes. Serve on a hot dish with a little hot gravy poured round.

Omelette Naturelle (Plain Omelet).

Beat up six fresh eggs with two tablespoonfuls of milk or cream, season with salt and very little pepper. Melt one ounce of butter in an omelet pan, and cook the omelet as above directed.

Omelette a l'Anglaise (English Omelet).

Prepare an omelet an above, adding two thru slices of streaky bacon, cut in strips and fried in butter, to the egg mixture, or else garnishing the omelet when made with thin slices of fried or grilled boom.

Omelette aux Fines Herbes {Savoury Omelet).

6 eggs,
1 tablespoonful cream,
2 dessertspoonfuls chopped parsley,
including a leaf or two of green tarragon and
a sprig of chervil,
a pinch of sweet herbs,
1 oz. butter,
a clove of garlic,
a pepper and salt.

Break the eggs into a basin, add the cream, beat up well, and add the chopped herbs and seasoning. Cut the clove of garlic and wipe the inside of the omelet-pan with the cut side. Melt the butter in this pan and when hot pour in the egg mixture. Stir over a brisk fire with a fork until the eggs begin to set, then roll towards the side of the pan opposite the handle and give it the shape of an oval cushion. Allow it to take colour (a golden brown). Turn out on an oval dish (hot), and serve. Tarragon and sweet herbs, or the flavour of garlic may be omitted. A small chopped shallot may be added to the butter and fried a little, if liked.

Omelette aux Asperger (Asparagus Omelet).

Cut into inch or half-inch lengths the soft portion of twenty-five to thirty heads of cleaned green asparagus. Blanch them and cook in salted water till tender, when done, drain them on a sieve, toss them in a little butter, add a little stock or white sauce, season with pepper and keep hot. Beat up six or seven eggs. Add a table-spoonful of milk or cream, salt and pepper to taste, and pour into an omelet pan containing 1½ oz. butter (melted)), stir over the fire until the eggs begin to set, shape to an oval cushion, placing the prepared asparagus in the centre, fold in the ends of the omelet, let it take colour, and turn out carefully on to a hot dish.

Omelette a la Bonne femine.

6 eggs,
1 oz bacon,
a boiled potato,
a breakfast roll,
1 teaspoonful chopped parsley,
½ teaspoonful chopped chives,
salt and pepper.

Break the eggs into a basin beat up for five minutes. Add the parsley and chives, also a pinch of salt and pepper to taste. Cut the bacon into small squares, likewise the thin crust of the roll, melt the butter in a frying- or omelet-pan. fry the bacon slightly brown, add the bread-crust and the potato cut into squares, toss over the fire fox a few minutes, pour in the egg mixture, and stir with a fork gently over a bright fire for two minutes. Fold up in the shape of a cushion towards the side opposite to the handle of the pan. hold it in a slanting position for a minute over the fire to colour it lightly: take a hot dish in the left hand, holding the pan with the right, bring the centre of the dish towards the edge of the pan with the omelet, and turn the pan over quickly so that the omelet will come right in the centre of the dish. Serve hot with two or three tablespoonfuls of tomato same poured round the dish.

Omelette a la Charentiere.

Beat up 6 eggs in a basin, add the necessary seasoning (pepper, salt, and nutmeg), a tablespoonful of milk or cream, and a heaped-up teaspoonful of French mustard. Cut two or three ounces of lean bacon into small dice, and fry in an omelet-pan with .an ounce of butter for a few minutes. Add two finely minced shallots and fry likewise, but do not allow them to get quite brown. Pour in the egg-mixture, and stir over a brisk fire till it commences to set. Then shape quickly into the form of .an oval cushion, allow it to take colour, and turn out on a hot dish.

Omelette a la Bernoise.

Proceed as above omitting the bacon and adding a about two ounces of gruyere cheese cut into small dice. Fry the shallots in an ounce and a half of butter. Pour in the mixture with cheese, and finish cooking in the usual manner.

Omelette a la Raphael

Make a savoury omelet with six eggs, place in the centre a fine stew of fillet of beef (goulash de beef) and truffles and fold the omelet. When browned slightly, turn on to a hot dish, and pour some demi-glace sauce round the base of the dish. Serve quickly.

Omelette aux PoIreaux (Leek Omelet).

6 eggs,
1½ oz butter,
1 tablespoonful grated cheese,
salt and cayenne,
1 tablespoonful milk or cream,
2 leeks, well washed, trimmed and stewed in brown sauce.

Break the eggs into a basin. Add the cheese, sufficient salt and cayenne to taste, and the milk or cream. Beat well to amalgamate the yolks and whites of eggs and other ingredients. Cut the cooked leeks into slices, and keep hot in a small stew-pan with just enough sauce to moisten. Melt the butter in an omelet-pan. When thoroughly warm (not too hot), pour in the egg mixture, and stir over a bright fire until the eggs begin to set. Shape quickly into the form of a cushion, place the stewed leeks in the centre and fold in the ends. Allow the omelet to take colour, then turn out on a hot dish. Pour a little brown sauce round the base of the dish and serve quickly.

Petites Omelettes a la Marechale.

8 eggs,
8 slices of cooked smoked ox-tongue,
a dessertspoonful of chopped parsley,
¼ gill of cream,
1½ oz butter,
salt,
pepper,
Colbert sauce.

Break the eggs into a basin. Add parsley, pepper, salt and beat up well, add the cream, and mix thoroughly. Divide into eight equal portions, melt a little of the butter, prepare a very small omelet with each portion of the mixture. Place it on a slice of tongue, trimmed to required size, and proceed thus until the eight omelets are made. Dish up on a hot dish in the shape of a border, pour Colbert sauce round the dish,   and serve.

Omelettes gratinees au Parmesan (Parmesan Omelet).

6 eggs,
1 large tablespoonful cream,
2 tablespoonful grated parmesan,
1½ oz. butter,
white pepper,
a few brown crumbs,
tomato sauce.

Break the eggs into a basin, add rather more than half of the grated cheese and a pinch of pepper (no salt). Mix well with a whisk. Add the cream, and beat well. Melt half the butter in an omelet-pan. Pour in half the egg mixture. Stir over a brisk fire until the eggs begin to set (it requires generally three minutes to stir), fold into a cushion shape, let it rest for one minute to take colour, and turn on to a hot dish. With the other half of the mixture and butter prepare a second omelet, and put it along with the first. Trim the omelets neatly, sprinkle over with a few breadcrumbs and grated parmesan, also a few drops of oiled butter, put the dish in a sharp oven or under a hot salamander for a few minutes and serve with nicely-seasoned hot tomato sauce poured round the omelets.

Omelettes Duchesse a l'Ecarlate (Small Omelets stuffed with Tongue).

8 eggs,
1 tablespoonful essence,
a tiny pinch of ground mace,
5 slices of toasted bread,
8 oz. minced chicken cooked,
mushroom and tongue trimmings for salpicon,
meat glaze,
3 tablespoonfuls cream,
1 tablespoonful grated cheese,
salt and pepper,
1 pinch paprika pepper,
5 slices of cooked tongue,
3 oz. fresh butter, truffles,

veloutee or other good white sauce for the salpicon,
demi-glace or Madere sauce.

Beat up the eggs in a basin, add the cream and chicken essence, and whisk till all ingredients are well amalgamated. Next stir in the cheese and seasoning. Make five small omelets of even size in the usual manner, using only just enough butter to keep the mixture from sticking to the pan. When ready for folding, place a tablespoonful of chicken salpicon in the centre of each, then fold and shape, let each take colour, and turn out on a slice of neatly-trimmed glazed ox-tongue. Place this on a similarly-cut slice of toasted and buttered bread. Proceed thus with the remaining four omelets. Glaze each with some dissolved meat glaze. Dish them up, pour some demi-glace or Madere sauce round the dish, and garnish with fresh parsley.

Omelette aux Huitres (Oyster Omelet).

8-10 large oysters,
1 tablespoonful cream or milk,
1 oz. butter,
5-6 eggs,
salt and pepper.

Cook the oysters in their own liquor, drain them and remove the beards, and cut into small dice, beat up the eggs and add the cream or stock, season to taste with salt and pepper; then add the oysters. Melt the butter in an omelet-pan, pour in the egg mixture, and stir over a quick fire till the eggs begin to set. Fold over and shape neatly (cushion shape), allow the omelet to take colour, and turn out into a hot dish.

Omelette a la Gordon.

Prepare a plain omelet simply seasoned with salt and pepper, before folding put in the centre a few slices of truffle and a few slices of beef-marrow, previously blanched and cooked in Madere sauce. Now fold and shape the omelet, let it set and take colour, and turn on to a hot dish. Pour a little Madere sauce round the base of the dish, and serve.

Omelette Savoyarde.

Beat up four to five eggs, add a dessertspoonful of grated cheese, and season with salt and pepper. Cut into small dice two cold potatoes, and fry in rather more than an ounce of butter in an omelet-pan, when nicely browned, stir in the eggs, etc., and shape into an omelet over a quick fire.

Omelet au Jambon (Ham Omelet).

Mince, not too finely, about 2 oz. of lean cooked ham, and mix with 6 well-beaten eggs, 1-2 tablespoonful of milk, and seasoning. Melt 1 oz. butter in an omelet-pan in the mixture, and finish as directed for savoury omelet (see recipe).

Omelette aux Anchois (Anchovy Omelet).

Prepare a plain omelet - Omelette Naturelle (see Recipe), adding one teaspoonful of anchovy sauce and three filleted gorgona anchovies, cut into small strips or dice, to the egg mixture, and cook as directed.

Omelette aux Sardines (Sardine Omelet).

Proceed the same as for anchovy omelet, using four boned and skinned sardines in place of the anchovies, but allowing the anchovy essence to be incorporated.

Omelette a l'Indienne (Curry Omelet).

Peel and mince finely half a small Spanish onion, fry it a light brown colour in one ounce of butter, add a dessertspoonful of curry powder and one tablespoonfnl of bechamel sauce. Cook for ten minutes, remove the fat, if any. Fill this into a plain omelet (Omelette Naturelle). Turn the omelet on a bed of boiled rice dressed on a hot dish, and surround with curry sauce.

Omelette au Homard (Lobster Omelet).

Prepare a plain omelet (Omelette Naturelle), fill it before folding in the sides with creamed lobster, or with minced lobster warmed up in a little bechamel sauce.

Omelette aux Oignons (Onion Omelet).

Proceed the same as for curry omelet, omitting the curry and rice. The onion can be cooked in white or brown sauce.

Omelette a la Bearnaise.

Prepare a plain omelet (Omelette Naturelle), fill it before turning in the sides with a mixture of artichoke bottoms and mushrooms cut into dice and heated up in tomato and bearnaise sauce. Pour a little sauce round the base of the dish.

Omelette a la Bayonne.

Prepare a plain omelet (Omelette Naturelle), fill it before folding in the sides with cooked ham and Spanish pimientos cut in strips and heated up in tomato sauce. Pour a little of the latter round the omelet.

Omelette a la Cervelle (Brain Omelet).

Prepare and cook a plain omelet (Omelette Naturelle) filled with cooked calf's brains cut in small pieces and stewed in seasoned white sauce.

Omelette aux Champignons (Mushroom Omelet).

Cut twelve to eighteen preserved mushrooms into slices, cook them in Madeira sauce. Fill into the centre of a plain omelet (Omelette Naturelle), fold in the sides, and turn out on a hot dish.

Omelette aux Concombres (Cucumher Omelet).

Peel half a cucumber, cut it in half lengthways, scoop out the seedy part, cut up into slices and stew in cream sauce. Fill with it a plain omelet (Omelette Naturelle).

Omelette aux Epinards (Spinach Omelet).

Rub half a pound of cooked spinach through a sieve. Heat it up with a little bechamel or brown sauce, season to taste, and fill into the centre of a plain omelet (Omelette Naturelle). Ponr a little gravy or brown sauce round the omelet.

Omelette au Fromage (Cheese Omelet).

Beat up six eggs with one ounce of grated gruyere cheese and two tablespoonfuls of milk. Melt one ounce of butter in an omelet pan and cook the omelet as directed for plain omelet. Sprinkle over the surface of the omelet with a little grated cheese.

Omelette au Lentilles (Lentil Omelet).

Fry two slices of nicely-minced onion in half an ounce of butter.

Put in one gill of cooked lentils, stir well, and add half a gill of brown sauce. Cook for ten minutes, and fill with it a plain or savoury omelet (see recipes "Omelette Naturelle" and "Omelette aux Fines Herbes").

Omelette aux Rognons (Kidney Omelet).

Slice thinly two small sheep's kidneys, season and dredge with flour, and fry in an omelet-pan containing half an ounce of butter and one finely-minced shallot fried lightly. Toss the kidneys in this over a quick fire for five minutes, add half a gill of Madere sauce, and cook for another five minutes. Make a plain omelet (Omelette Naturelle), fill the above in the centre of it, fold in carefully, and turn out on a hot dish,

Omelette aux Tomates (Tomato Omelet).

Steep two or three small ripe tomatoes in hot water and skin them. Cut them into slices and toss them in a little butter over a quick fire, season well, and fill with it a plain or savoury omelet (see recipes "Omelette Naturelle" and "Omelette aux Fines Herbes"). Pour a little tomato sauce round the base of the dish,

Omelette aux Truffles (Truffle Omelet).

Proceed the same as for mushroom omelet (see Omelette aux Champignons recipe), using six truffles in place of the mushrooms.

Omelette Soufflees au Poisson (Fish Puff Omelet).

Shred finely one small cooked whiting or a slice of cooked cod, heat it up in a little butter, and season to taste. Stir this into a mixture made as directed below, and bake in a well-buttered pan in a fairly hot oven for about twenty minutes. Turn out into a hot dish, and serve with tomato sauce.

Omelette Souffle aux fines herbes (Savoury Puff Omelet).

Beat up lightly the yolks of six eggs and whisk stiffly the whites of three, stir into the former one tablespoonful cornflour mixed with ½ gill of cream or milk, season with salt and pepper, and stir in one teaspoonful of finely chopped parsley ; add the whites of egg last of all. Melt half an ounce of butter in a buttered souffle dish or omelet pan, pour in the mixture, and set the pan into a hot oven. When it thickens add the remaining whites of eggs, well whisked with a pinch of salt, and return to oven until a delicate brown. Turn it out on to a hot dish, or send to table in the souffle dish, if such is used. Serve at once.

SOUFFLE OMELET DISH

PLATS D'OEUFS— EGG DISHES.

Oeufs poches au Vin blanc (Poached Eggs in White Wine).

Poach carefully six to eight eggs in slightly salted water flavoured with white wine and a few drops of lemon-juice. Have ready as many fried bread croutons as there are poached eggs. Take up the eggs, trim them neatly, and place them on the croutons, then dish up. Have ready a sauce prepared with one gill of reduced white wine, an ounce and a half of meat glaze, and one ounce of butter The latter must be whisked in in very small quantities, and must not boil. Season with a good pinch of cayenne or krona pepper. Mask the eggs with the sauce, which must be thick enough to coat them nicely, sprinkle a little chopped parsley over each egg, and serve.

Oeufs aux Nouilles a la Carola.

Prepare some nouille paste (see recipe), cut it into very thin strips, and blanch in salted water for three minutes, drain and toss in butter. Season with nutmeg and pepper, and put some on a buttered fireproof dish. Dredge well with grated cheese. Upon this range a layer of slices of hard-boiled eggs, then a layer of nouilles, and lastly a layer of fresh mushrooms, seasoned, and tossed in butter. Cover with a well-reduced bechamel sauce, strew with grated cheese and oiled butter. Bake in a sharp oven for ten minutes.

Oeufs a la Suzette.

Cut some baked potatoes in halves lengthwise, scoop out the mealy part and mix with bechamel sauce, grated cheese, and seasoning. Line the potato crusts with this and put in each a poached egg (neatly trimmed). Spread some of the mixture over each, and sprinkle with cheese and breadcrumbs and oiled butter. Bake in a sharp oven and serve hot.

Oeufs a la Princesse (Egg Darioles).

4 to 6 eggs,

1 oz. grated parmesan cheese,
2 oz. butter,
a haudlul cooked asparagus points,
preserved lax,
salt,
paprika pepper,
tomato sauce,
toasted bread.

Butter four to six small dariole moulds, sprinkle with grated cheese and a few pinches of paprika pepper, break an egg carefully into each mould, and season with pepper and salt. Place the moulds in a saute-pan, containing enough hot water to reach half-way up the mould, and cook on the stove or in the oven until the whites of the eggs are set. Stamp out some rounds or ovals of toasted bread about the size of an egg, butter them well on one side, and lay a slice of lax on each. Toss the asparagus points in a little butter, season to taste, and put in layers on the buttered toast. Turn out the moulds on top of the asparagus, dish up, garnish with sprigs of parsley, and serve with a sauce-boat of tomato sauce.

Fricassee d'Oeufs (Fricasseed Eggs).

6 eggs,
1½ oz. butter,
1 gill cream,
½ gill bechamel sauce,
a small shallot,
pepper,
salt,
a pinch of grated nutmeg,
fried bread croutons,
a teaspoonful of chopped parsley.

Boil the eggs for fifteen minutes, lay them in cold water, take off the shells, cut them in halves crosswise, take out the yolks for garnish. Peel the shallot and chop finely. Melt the butter in a stew-pan, add the shallot, and fry a golden colour. Add the sauce, let it come to the boil, mix in the cream, when hot put in the whites of eggs, add the seasoning. Stir gently, or, better, shake the pan so as not to break the slices, and keep on the fire until hot. Warm up the yolks in a little thin white sauce, dress them in the centre of a dish, put the whites round the yolks as neatly as possible, sprinkle over with some chopped parsley, garnish with a few croutons of fried bread, and serve.

Oeufs a la Dreux.

6 eggs,
¼ lb. lean ham (cooked),
1 dessertspoonful chopped parsley,
½ oz. butter,
½ gill cream,
salt and pepper,
cayenne,
six rounds of buttered toast.

Butter thickly six deep patty-pans, chop the ham finely and mix with the parsley, sprinkle well the patty-pans with this, so as to completely cover the inside of each pan, break an egg carefully into each pan, season with a pinch of salt, pepper, and cayenne. Divide the cream equally on top of each egg, and put a tiny piece of butter in each. Put the tins in a saute-pan three-parts full of boiling water, place in the oven, and poach until the whites are completely set. Have ready some rounds of buttered toast as nearly as possible the size of the patty-pans, turn out the eggs and dress them carefully on the toast, dish up, and serve very hot.

Oeufs a la Milanaise.

6 eggs,
3 tablespoonfuls grated parmesan cheese,
1 tablespoonful cream,

toasted bread,
pepper,
about ½ gill tomato sauce,
1½ oz. butter.

Break the eggs into a basin, beat up well with a tablespoonful of grated parmesan cheese and the cream, add a pinch of pepper. Divide this into four equal parts. Melt a little butter in an omelet-pan, pour in one part and make into a small omelet, taking care that the omelet is of a nice cushion shape. Proceed thus until four omelets are made. Roll each in parmesan cheese, put them on oval shapes of buttered toast, sprinkle the surface with more parmesan, put them on a baking-sheet, and place in a hot oven for two minutes. Dish up on a hot dish, pour round some hot tomato sauce and serve.

Oeufs a la Boston.

6 eggs,
1½ oz. butter,
½ large onion,
1 teaspoonful flour,
1 gill milk or cream,
2 oz. chopped cooked ham,
salt,
pepper,
nutmeg,
½ gill Madere sauce.

Peel and slice the onion, fry it in an ounce of butter to a golden colour, sprinkle in the flour, stir long enough to cook the flour, moisten with the milk or cream, season with a pinch of salt and half a pinch each of pepper and nutmeg. Separate the yolks from the whites of eggs and put the yolks with the onions, etc., stir well, and add one ounce of chopped ham. Beat the whites of eggs to a stiff froth and mix carefully with the above. Butter a round baking-tin or gratin-dish, dress the mixture neatly on it, sprinkle the top with chopped ham, bake in a hot oven for fifteen minutes, when done, turn out on a hot dish, and serve with Madere sauce.

Oeufs brouilles (Scrambled Eggs).

6 eggs,
½ gill cream,
¾ oz. butter,
salt and pepper to taste,
toasted bread (buttered).

Break the eggs into a basin, add pepper and salt, beat with a fork until the yolks and whites are thoroughly mixed. Put it in a stew-pan with the butter and cream, stir over a brisk fire until the mixture begins to set. Have ready a square piece of toasted bread well buttered, cut each into quarters, put neatly on a hot dish, turn the egg mixture on to this, garnish with a few sprigs of fresh parsley, and serve. Or, instead of dressing the eggs on toast, put the mixture, heaped up, in the centre of a dish, and garnish with sippets of toasted bread.

Oeufs brouilles aux Pointes d'Asperges.

6 eggs,
1 gill asparagus tips,
2 oz. butter,
1 tablespoonful cream,
salt,
pepper,
nutmeg.

Boil the asparagus tips in salted water until tender, drain well, put them in a saute-pan with an ounce of melted butter, and saute over the fire for five minutes. Break the eggs in a basin, add the cream, season with a little salt, a pinch of pepper, and a grate of nutmeg, beat up well, put it in a stew-pan with the remaining ounce of butter, stir over the fire for a little while, then add the asparagus, and stir again until the eggs begin to set. Dish up on a hot dish, garnish with parsley, and serve. Slices of cucumber in place of asparagus points will be found a nice change. pinch of castor sugar should be added when sauteing, if cucumber is used.

Oeufs brouilles aux Anchois (Anchovy Buttered Eggs).

6 eggs,
1 teaspoonful anchovy essence,
1½ oz. butter,
2 tablespoonfuls cream,
6 gorgona anchovies,
a pinch of cayenne pepper and salt,
toasted slices of bread,
parsley for garnish.

Wipe the anchovies with a damp cloth, remove the fillets, and cut into strips. Cut the toast in oblong slices about three inches long and two inches broad, and butter them. Beat up the eggs, put them, together with the anchovy essence, an ounce of butter and the cream in a small stew-pan, add a pinch of cayenne, and salt to taste. Stir over the fire until the mixture begins to set, put an equal quantity on the buttered side of each j)iece of toast, lay the strips, of anchovies across each in the shape of lattice-work, place a caper in each cavity, dish up, put the dish in the oven for a few minutes, garnish with parsley, and serve hot.

Oeufs brouilles aux Trufles (Scrambled Eggs with Truffles).

6 eggs,
1½ oz. butter,

1 large trutfle,
½ glass marsala,
salt,
pepper,
nutmeg,
1 slice toasted bread.

Cut the truffles into fine shreds, put them in a stew-pan with the wine and a tiny piece of butter, cover and reduce the liquid to about half its quantity. Break the eggs into a basin, season with salt, pepper, and a pinch of grated nutmeg, mix thoroughly. Melt the butter in a stew-pan, pour in the eggs, stir over the tire until the mixture begins to set, then add the truffle, etc., quickly. Mix well together, stir over the tire for another minute, then turn on a hot dish on a slice of buttered toast, dress in a heap, garnish with a few sippets of toast, and serve.

Note . — Cooked ham, tongue, mushrooms, peas, asparagus points, etc., may be used as a change, in place of the truffles, but for cooked vegetables the wine should be omitted and replaced with cream.

Oeufs brouilles a la Turque (Eggs, Turkish Style).

Break six to eight eggs into a basin, season with pepper and salt and a teaspoonful of chopped parsley. Whisk them well, stir into a stew-pan containing an ounce of melted butter, stir over the fire till the eggs are set enough to be turned out, then dress them in the form of a border on a hot round dish. Have ready a saute of chicken livers (finely sliced and tossed in butter, flavoured with shallot and parsley, and suitably seasoned), put these in the centre of the dish, pour some hot tomato sauce round the base of the dish and send to table immediately.

Oeufs garnis a la Coquette.

6-8 new-laid eggs,
1 oz. butter,
about ½ gill cream,
3 oz. lean ham or tongue,
salt,
cayenne,
nutmeg.

Procure six-eight small china souffle cases, butter them well, put a small piece of butter in each of them, also a tablespoonful of ream, a pinch of salt, and a little grated nutmeg, place them on a baking-sheet in a hot oven or on the top of the stove. When the contents commence to simmer, break carefully into each one egg, put a tiny pinch of cayenne pepper in the centre of each yolk, put back on the stove or in the oven, and allow the eggs to set lightly. Have ready the ham or tongue finely chopped, sprinkle over the white part, so as to leave the yolks free, serve very hot.

Oeufs Miroire a la Princesse.

6 eggs,
6 rounds fried bread,
1 oz. butter,
2 oz. cooked ham or tongue,
parsley,
the yolk of a hard-boiled egg,
asparagus-point ragout,
salt and pepper.

Melt the butter in a saute-pan, break the eggs one by one into a basin and slide them into the pan, and cook them in the oven until the whites are set, season lightly with white pepper and salt. Cut them out with a plain round cutter and place each on a crouton of fried bread. Ornament the eggs with alternate little groups of chopped ham or tongue, chopped parsley, and chopped yolk of egg (hard-boiled). Dress them neatly on a round dish, put them in the oven just a second or two, fill the centre with a ragout of cooked asparagus points and serve.

Oeufs farcis aux Crevettes (Stuffed Eggs with Prawns).

4 hard-boiled eggs,
12 large or 18 small prawns,
3 gorgona anchovies,
1½ oz. butter,
1 tablespoonful bechamel sauce,
salt,
pepper,
cayenne,
1 gill tomato sauce.

Remove the shell from the eggs, cut them in halves crosswise, scoop out the yolks and put them in a mortar, add the boned anchovies and picked prawns, and pound very line. Rub all through a wire sieve, return to the mortar, add the butter and bechamel sauce, mix thoroughly, and season to taste. Fill up the hard-boiled whites of egg, place a prawn-head in the centre of each, sprinkle the surface with a little grated parmesan cheese, put them on a buttered dish or saute-pan, and bake in a hot oven for about ten minutes. Dish up neatly, sauce round with hot tomato sauce, and serve.

Oeufs a la Carnot.

Trim neatly some artichoke bottoms of a nice white colour, cut the edges into a fancy border, keep warm in some dissolved meat glaze. Have ready some rather thick chicken puree, blended with a little fresh butter over the fire. Poach a new-laid egg for each fond, put a tablespoonful of chicken puree in the fond, trim the eggs nicely, place on top, dish up, sauce over with gravy, and serve.

Croquettes aux Oeufs (Egg Croquettes).

Cut six to eight hard-boiled eggs into slices, rub them through a coarse wire sieve. Mince coarsely a dozen preserved mushrooms, and slightly fry them in an ounce of butter. To this add the egg puree, stir well, season with salt, pepper, and a grate of nutmeg. Moisten with sufficient well-reduced bechamel sauce to form a binding. When thoroughly hot, pour the mixture on a plate and let it cool. Shape the mixture into croquettes, even-sized balls, or cork shapes, dip each into beaten egg, and cover well with coarse-grained florador or semolina, the former is preferable. Fry in hot fat a golden colour, dish up neatly, and garnish with fried parsley.

Note . — The above, dressed around a bed of cooked spinach, nicely seasoned, makes a very tasty dinner or supper dish.

Cromesquis aux Oeufs (Kromeskies of Eggs).

3 hard-boiled eggs,
2 raw yolks of eggs,
¼ gill bechamel sauce,
½ teaspoonful finely chopped truffle,
½ oz. chopped ox-tongue,
5 thin pancakes (unsweetened) or bacon,
seasoning,
frying-batter,
frying-fat.

Peel the eggs, cut them into slices, and chop rather coarsely, put them in a stew-pan, moisten with the sauce and the egg-yolks, season to taste with pepper, salt, and nutmeg. Stir over the fire till hot, add the truffles and tongue, mix well, and turn on to a plate to cool. Shape into even-sized corks, wrap each in a square piece of pancake or bacon, dip into frying batter, and fry in hot fat. Drain, dish up on a folded napkin, and garnish with crisp parsley.

Oeufs en Chaud-froid.

6 or more new-laid eggs,
1½ gill bechamel sauce,
½ gill tomato sauce,
1 gill aspic jelly,
¼ oz. leaf gelatine,
1 large truffle,
slices of cooked ox-tongue or ham,
salad and dressing.

Poach the eggs carefully in slightly salted water containing a little lemon-juice, when set take up and trim and set them on a sieve to cool. Heat up the white sauce, add to it the gelatine, previously dissolved and strained. Season the dish to taste. Mix with a couple of tablespoonfuls of aspic. When nearly cold mask half the number of poached eggs. This must be done twice, allowing the first coating to set before the second one is added. Now heat up the tomato sauce and mix in an equal quantity of white sauce and some aspic jelly, when nearly cold, mask the remainder of eggs in the same manner. Cut out as many rounds of tongue or ham as there are eggs, the slices should be as near as possible the size of the eggs. Place one egg on each slice, mask them over with a thin coating of aspic, decorate tastefully with fancifully-cut slices of truffle. Dish up on a cold dish in the form of a border, fill the centre of a dish with a nicely prepared salad, and serve.

Oeufs a la Colbert.

Take four or six new-laid eggs. Break each very carefully in a cup, season with pepper and salt, sprinkle over about half a teaspoonful of grated gruyere or parmesan cheese, and drop each very gently into a pan of hot fat or frying oil, the latter, if of good quality, is preferable for this purpose. Keep the eggs in shape, and turn frequently by means of a wooden spoon. Fry them to a pretty golden colour, then take up and drain them on a cloth or kitchen paper. Dress them neatly on a hot dish, sprinkle over with grated cheese, and serve quickly.

Oeufs frits au Beurre noir (Fried Eggs in Brown Butter).

Melt an ounce of butter in an earthenware fireproof pan (casserole), when hot break into it gently three or four eggs, have ready three or four rounds of buttered toast a little larger than the eggs, spread them with a little anchovy paste, take up the eggs one at a time, trim into a neat, round shape, and place them on the toast. Reheat the butter remaining in the casserole, and let it get a dark nut-brown colour (not black), then add a dessertspoonful of tarragon vinegar and a good pinch of chopped parsley or chives, reduce a little, pour over the eggs on the dish and serve.

Oeufs a la Parmentier.

3 large potatoes,
6 small eggs,
1 gill white cream sauce (bechamel or supreme),

1 oz. grated cheese,
½ oz. butter,
breadcrumbs.

Wash and scrub the potatoes, dry them, bake them in the oven, cut them into halves, and scoop out the mealy parts. Poach the eggs in slightly salted water, flavoured with lemon-juice, trim them, put a little sauce in each half of the potatoes, place an egg in each, mix the remainder of sauce with half the cheese, cover the eggs with the sauce, sprinkle with breadcrumbs and grated cheese, divide the butter into little bits and place on top, and brown in a very hot oven. Dish up, and serve quickly.

Oeufs a l'Ecarlate (Poached Eggs with Tongue).

6 new-laid eggs,
6 slices of cooked ox-tongue,
1 gill gravy or rich brown stock,
1 small glass sherry or marsala,
salt,
pepper,
lemon-juice,
about 1½ gill supreme sauce.

Poach the eggs in boiling water, slightly salted and flavoured with lemon-juice. Cut the slices of tongue into neat shapes, about the size of the egg, when poached. Chop the trimmings of tongue very finely. Put the slices of tongue in a saute-pan with the gravy and wine, and heat up thoroughly. Take up the eggs, drain and trim them, place each upon a slice of tongue, arrange on a hot dish, season with salt and pepper, sauce over carefully with hot supreme sauce, and serve hot. Put a little chopped tongue in the centre of each egg.

Oeufs a la Courbet (Cold).

Cut some even-sized ripe tomatoes in halves, scoop out carefully the interior, and fill with scrambled egg, nicely seasoned. When cold, mask carefully with a stiff mayonnaise and a thin layer of aspic jelly. Dish up in a circle, garnish with gherkins and pickled beetroot cut into fanciful shapes, and fill the centre of the dish with lettuce and tomatoes cut into julienne strips, suitably seasoned with an oil and vinegar dressing. Serve cold.

Oeufs frits a la Fermiere.

Grill or broil eight thin slices of lean bacon or ham, fry the same number of eggs in a little butter or bacon fat, trim each neatly and place on a slice of bacon or ham. Range these in the form of a border round a dish, fill the centre with a mixture of vegetables (macedoine de legumes) heated and mixed with a little white sauce. Garnish the centre with Parisian potatoes (marble-shaped potatoes, blanched, drained, and baked in the oven or fried). The dish is then ready for serving.

Oeufs poches a la Tomate (Poached Eggs, Tomato Sauce).

Boil up a pint of tomato sauce in a saute-pan, skim it if necessary, and drop in carefully five or six eggs, cook them till the white is firm to the touch, basting the eggs well with the sauce during this process. Lift them carefully with a slice or skimmer, trim them, dish up on pieces of toasted bread. Pour over the sauce, which must be suitably seasoned with salt and pepper, and serve hot.

Oeufs en Matelote (Eggs, Seaman's Way).

Poach some eggs in a rich meat stock, trim them and dress them on rounds of buttered toast, sauce over with a ricli brown sauce flavoured with savoury herbs and finely minced fried onion. Garnish with strips of fillets of anchovies.

Pyramide d'Oeufs a la Reforme.

These are stuffed halves of hard-boiled eggs, dished up in a pyramidal form, sprinkled over with finely shredded ham and truffles. Sauce over with a rich brown sauce, and bake in a quick oven.

Oeufs a la Garfield.

These are very similar to Scotch eggs. Take some hard-boiled ggs, remove the shells, and cover them with a layer of farce or sausage meat, egg and crumb them with crushed vermicelli, fry in deep fat or clarified butter, cut in halves, and serve with piquante sauce.

Oeufs a la Messina.

Toss in fresh butter as many artichoke bottoms (preserved) as may be required, and drain them. Poach carefully the same number of eggs, and trim them. Range the artichoke bottoms in the form of a border on a round dish, and place a poached egg in each. Mask the whole with a well-reduced bordelaise sauce, put a thin slice of cooked beef-marrow and a slice of truffle in the centre of each egg. Sprinkle with chopped parsley, and serve hot.

Oeufs a la Carigen.

Poach carefully six to eight new-laid eggs, drain them well, and stamp out each with a round cutter. Reduce half a pint of rich bechamel, into which incorporate a tablespoonful of grated parmesan cheese and three yolks of eggs. Mask each egg with this sauce. When set and cold, egg and crumb them twice. Fry them in deep fat, drain, and dish up on a hot dish covered with a lace-paper or napkin. Garnish with fried parsley, and serve with a boat of tomato sauce.

Oeufs a la Gagnor (Cold).

Take four or five hard-boiled eggs, cut them in halves crossways, cut a small piece off the end of each to make them stand, remove the yolks and fill the cavities with Russian caviare. Pound the yolks and mix with an ounce of fresh butter, a pinch of cayenne or paprika pepper, rub it through a sieve, and put it in a forcing-bag with a fancy tube. Decorate each half of egg tastefully with the butter, etc., place them on small croutons of fried bread, fixed on with a little of the puree. Dish up, and garnish with fancifully-cut slices of lemon and parsley.

Oeufs poches a la Reine (Poached Eggs, Queen's Style).

Mince rather finely half a pound or more of cold cooked chicken or turkey, freed from skin, bone, and gristle. Fry this in a little butter, and moisten with sufficient bechamel sauce to form a light salpicon. Keep hot. Poach in slightly salted water six new-laid eggs, trim them neatly. Put the mince in a round dish, and place the eggs neatly upon this. Glaze them with liquefied meat glaze or Lemco, and surround the dish with eight small half-moon shaped slices of bread fried in clarified butter. Garnish with sprigs of parsley, and serve hot.

Oeufs St. Jacques (Eggs, St. James's Style).

Line eight to nine small bouche moulds with puff-paste or rough puff-paste (roll out the paste rather thinly, and stamp out the rounds necessary for lining with a fluted cutter). Prick the bottom of the paste with a fork. Fill them with rice or dried peas, and bake them in a moderate oven to a golden colour. Unmould whilst hot. Brush over the outside and inside with beaten yolk of egg mixed with meat glaze, and return to the oven for a few minutes, then let cool. Poach, in smaller-sized bouche moulds than those first used, as many eggs as are necessary. Unmould them and let cool, then mask them with aspic, and set each in one of the prepared crusts. Decorate with chopped aspic tinted with a little spinach greening. Dish np tastefully, and serve cold.

Oeufs a la Medicis.

Drain a handful of slices of pickled beetroot on a cloth, and saute them in a saute-pan with fresh butter over a moderate fire. To this add four hard-boiled eggs cut into slices, season with pepper and salt, add a good teaspoonful of chopped parsley and moisten with half a gill of cream, cover the pan and place it in the oven for about ten minutes. Dish up neatly, and serve hot.

Oeufs a l'Indienne (Curried Eggs).

4 eggs,
1 oz. butter,
¾ oz. flour,
½ onion,
½ apple,
2 teaspoonfuls curry powder,
1½ gill stock,
salt,
boiled rice.

Boil the eggs ten minutes, shell them, and put into a basin of cold water, then cut two of the eggs into four rounds, and each round into two, cut np small the other eggs. Peel the apple and onion, and chop each finely. Melt the butter in a saucepan, and fry the onion and apple a golden brown. Put in the curry powder, flour, and a little salt, stir over a fire a few minutes, then add the stock gradually, and simmer gently about ten minutes. Put in the chopped pieces of egg, and allow to get hot. Turn the curry on to a hot dish, arrange the sliced egg round it, and a small border of boiled rice.

Oeufs en Feuilletage (Eggs in Puff-pastry).

5 hard-boiled eggs,
½ lb. puff-paste,
1 raw egg,
pepper and salt,

breadcrunibs,
clarified butter or lard for frying.

Remove the shells from the eggs when hard, mix a little white pepper with some hue dry salt, roll four eggs in this. Roll out the puff-paste about one-eighth of an inch thick, wrap up each egg in the paste, brush the edges of the paste so as to close the ends securely, egg and breadcrumb over twice, place them in a wire basket, and fry in hot butter or lard a nice light brown (this must be done very carefully to ensure the paste getting done through). Cut some rings about a quarter of an inch thick of the remaining hard-boiled egg. Take out the yolk, put each fried egg on a ring so that they may stand upright; dish up in a circle on a napkin; fry a handful of picked, washed, and dried parsley in the centre, and serve.

Oeufs a la Tripe.

Make a rich onion sauce, and add a gill of cream. Boil four to six eggs hard, shell them and cut up into slices, heat these up in the sauce. Dish up, and sprinkle with finely chopped parsley.

Oeufs mollets a la Bechamel.

Boil six new-laid eggs in water for five minutes. Shell them and place them on fried croutons of bread, pour some rich bechamel sauce over them. Dish up carefully and serve.

Oeufs au Beurre Noisette.

Melt half an ounce of bntter in a fireproof dish, break four to five eggs into it. Place in a hot oven for about five minutes. Then pour over half an ounce of butter cooked to a nut-brown colour with a dash of tarragon or chilli vinegar. Sprinkle with a few fried breadcrumbs and send to table.

Oeufs a la Waldimir.

Carefully break six fresh eggs into a buttered fireproof dish, cover with chopped truffles and asparagus points, seasoned. Add a little grated parmesan cheese, bake slightly in the oven, and send to table with supreme sauce poured round the base of the dish.

Cotelettes aux Oeufs (Egg Cutlets).

Mince not too finely some hard-boiled eggs, prepare with these a salpicon by adding grated cheese and herb seasoning, raw yolks, and white sauce, reheat and let cool, then shape into cutlets, egg and crumb them carefully, and fry in deep fat.

Ragout d'Oeufs a la Francaise.

Slices of hard-boiled eggs, with truffles and morels or mushrooms, stewed in brown sauce flavoured with lemon-juice and fine herbs.

Oeufs en Cocottes.

6 to 8 eggs,
 a little butter,
1 tablespoonful finely chopped parsley,
6 to 8 dessertspoonfuls cream.

Butter six to eight small fireproof pipkin pans, and sprinkle with chopped parsley. Break an egg carefully into each, with a dessertspoonful of cream. Bake slowly till set. Dish up and serve in the pipkin pans.

PIPKIN PAN

Oeufs brouilles a l'Italienne (Italian Scrambled Eggs).

Scrambled eggs placed in centre of a risotto border, i.e. cooked savoury rice mixed with fried chicken livers; a little tomato sauce poured round the base of the dish.

Oeufs brouilles an Jambon.

Scrambled eggs mixed with finely-shredded or minced ham.

Oeufs a la Creole.

Rounds of toasted and buttered bread spread with chicken cream, slightly poached eggs placed on each, and finished cooking in the oven; bechamel sauce poured round base of dish.

Oeufs a la Mode de Caen.

Slices of hard-boiled eggs, cooked in a rich white cream sauce, with slices of fried Spanish onion.

Oeufs a la Carmelite.

Halves of hard-boiled eggs stuffed with fried chopped shallots, parsley, sorrel, and yolks of eggs, and baked in the oven.

Oeufs a la Chipolata,

Cassolettes of bread, shaped to take the size of eggs, fried, and filled with poached eggs; garnished with braised button mushrooms, button onions, dice of ham, chestnuts, small fried sausages, and fried Parisian potatoes. Sauce Madere poured round the base of dish.

Oeufs a la Comtesse.

Poached eggs dressed on croutons of toasted or fried bread, sauced over with hollandaise, and chopped truffle on top).

Oeufs a la Creme de Volaille.

Egg-shells filled with a light chicken cream, and poached in stock. Top of egg-shells cut off, dished up, and garnished with a slice of truffle on each.

Oeufs a la Coque en Surprise (Cold).

Fresh eggs are carefully emptied, and refilled with scrambled egg mixture, blended, when cold, with mayonnaise, dressed on a bed of crisp celery shreds or endive.

Oeufs a la Pache.

Hard-boiled eggs sliced, mixed with mushroom heads, and heated up in tomato sauce, dressed in the centre of a rice border.

Oeufs a la Pasqual (Cold).

Small eggs poached in seasoned milk, trimmed, drained, and masked with chaud-froid sauce; when cold, dressed in a nest made of baked nouilles, and, if liked, a fish farce foundation.

Oeufs poches a l'Imperiale (Cold).

Poached eggs dressed on artichoke bottoms; garnisbed with macedoine of vegetables and julienne of tongue and tomatoes; sauced over with remoulade sauce.

ABBREVIATED RECIPES FOR OTHER EGG DISHES.

Oeufs a l'Americaine.
Shelled, soft-boiled eggs, ranged on a bed of chou-croute and sliced ham; sauce Madere.

Oeufs a l'Ancienne.
Poached eggs, with grilled mushrooms and grilled tomatoes; tomato sauce poured round.

Oeufs a l'Andalouse (Cold).

Poached eggs, coated with mayonnaise aspic, placed in halves of tomatoes, and decorated with aspic cubes and anchovy fillets.

Oeufs a l'Arlequin.

Poached eggs, dressed in fried bread croustades, covered with shredded ham and truffle and chopped parsley; gravy or demi-glace sauce.

Oeufs a l'Aumale.

Scrambled eggs, placed in centre of a border of sauteed kidneys; tomato sauce.

Oeufs a l'Aurore.

Poached eggs, placed in rounds of pastry rings, coated with aurore sauce.

Oeufs a la Bearnaise.

Hard-boiled eggs, sliced and heated up in rich bechamel sauce, dished up, coated with grated parmesan cheese, and browned in oven.

Oeufs a la Bedford.

Eggs cooked in cocotte pans or cases lined with a puree of calf's liver and cream, and covered with chopped tongue and truffle.

Oeufs a la Belle-Helene.

Poached eggs, sauced over with supreme sauce, and garnished with asparagus croquettes.

Oeufs a la Benedictine.
Poached eggs, dressed on egg-shaped croustades of puff pastry, previously lined with a puree of salt cod (morue), coated with rich cream sauce and chopped truffle.

Oeufs a la Bercy.
Eggs fried in butter on plates, garnished with slices of fried sausages; tomato sauce.

Oeufs a la Bohemienne.
Poached eggs on fried bread croutons, coated with bechamel sauce, and covered with finely chopped ham.

Oeufs a la Bouchere.
Poached eggs placed on oval-shaped bread or pastry crusts, coated with rich cream sauce blended with beef marrow and chopped parsley.

Oeufs a la Bourguignonne.
Scrambled eggs, mixed with sauteed escargots (edible vineyard snails), cut into dice, and strips of fried bacon slightly flavoured with garlic and parsley.

Oeufs a la Brebant.
Poached eggs placed on rounds of puff-pastry crust, lined with foie-gras and quail puree, and coated with truffle sauce.

Oeufs a la Bresilienne.
Scrambled eggs, dressed on croustades (pastry or bread, previously lined with anchovy puree) coated alternately, sauced over with tomato puree.

Oeufs a la Bretonne.
Poached eggs, dressed on a bed of haricot puree, coated with cream sauce.

Oeufs a la Bruxelloise.
Poached eggs, dressed on croutons on a dish, then covered with a puree of Brussels sprouts, breaded and browned under a salamander.

Oeufs a la Careme.
Hard-boiled eggs, cut into round slices, mixed with sliced truffle and artichoke bottoms, moistened with bechamel sauce, breaded and browned in the oven.

Oeufs a la Cardinal.
Poached eggs placed on to oval croustades, previously lined with lobster salpicon, mixed with truffles and mushrooms coated with sauce Cardinal.

Oeufs a la Chantilly.
Poached eggs placed on to tartlet crusts containing puree of green peas, coated over with green mousseline sauce.

Oeufs a la Chasseur.
Halves of hard-boiled eggs, farced with egg-yolk and game puree, served with poivrade sauce.

Oeufs a la Chivry.
Poached eggs on puff-pastry crusts, filled with spinach and watercress puree; sauce Chivry.

Oeufs a la Clamart.
Poached eggs on tartlet crust, garnished with green peas and finely shredded braised lettuce, sauced over with cream herb sauce.

Oeufs a la Cluny.
Fried eggs (sur plat), dished up on a bed of green peas, and garnished with small chicken croquettes; tomato sauce.

Oeufs a la Colombine.
Poached eggs, dressed on paste croustades, garnished with asparagus points and shredded truffles, sauced over with supreme sauce.

Oeufs a la Conde.
Eggs fried (sur plat), ranged on cooked red haricot beans, mixed with finely fried shredded bacon; sauce Bordeaux.

Oeufs a la Crecy.
Poached eggs placed on pastry croustades filled with rich carrot puree, and coated with cream sauce.

Oeufs a la Czarina (Cold).
Hard-boiled eggs hollowed out, filled with caviare, and placed on to croutons dished up (crown shape), masked with cardinal sauce, decorated and coated with aspic, with smoked salmon slices and anchovy fillets, and Russian salad ranged in centre of dish.

Oeufs a la Diable.

Fried eggs (sur plat), fried on both sides, sauced over with brown butter (beurre noir) well flavoured with chilli vinegar and cayenne.

Oeufs a la Duchesse.

Poached eggs placed on to potato cassolettes or croustades, sauced over with veloutee cream.

Oeufs a la Elisabeth.

Eggs poached and placed on to artichoke bottoms, sprinkled with minced truffles, coated with Mornay sauce and grated cheese browned in the oven.

Oeufs a l'Espagnole.

Scrambled eggs filled into hollowed-out tomatoes, previously fried in oil, and garnished with fried onion rings.

Oeufs a la Florentine.

Poached eggs on hollowed-out bread croutons, previously filled with spinach puree, coated with Mornay sauce sprinkled with parmesan cheese, and browned in oven.

Oeufs a la Forestiere.

Savoury eggs moulded and steamed, dished on brioche croustades.

Oeufs a la Gambetta.

Poached eggs, sprinkled with chopped parsley, each placed on fried egg, surmounted by a slice of truffle garnished with choron sauce.

Oeufs a la Hongroise.
Sliced hard-boiled eggs, dressed with alternate slices of tomatoes; bechamel sauce, paprika, and grated cheese, coated with white sauce, breaded and browned in the oven.

Oeufs a la Hussarde.
Poached eggs placed in halves of tomatoes, previously filled with duxelle and ham puree, sauced over with veloutee, highly seasoned.

Oeufs a la Khedive.
Poached eggs, dressed in tartlet paste crust, previously filled with chicken puree, garnished with spinach and chopped hard eggs; sauce veloutee.

Oeufs a la Lorette.
Poached eggs, neatly dressed on rings made of potato puree, like croquettes, garnished with asparagus points and egg-rings, decorated with truffles; gravy or demi-glace sauce.

Oeufs a la Lucullus.
Cocotte pans, lined with foie-gras puree, then each filled with raw egg, a little truffle, and Madere sauce added, then poached in the oven.

Oeufs a la Mireille.
Oval-shaped bread croutons fried in oil, filled with savoury rice (saffron flavoured), with poached egg on each crouton, sauced over with paprika sauce, dish garnished with delicate tomato stew.

Oeufs a la Monaco.

Poached eggs, coated with lobster sauce, then glazed, and ecorated with small fried lobst^ escallops or cutlets.

Oeufs a la Mornay.

Poached eggs on toast, coated with Mornay sauce, breaded with cheese, and slightly browned in the oven.

Oeufs a la Mosaique (Cold).

Poached eggs, masked, when cold, with white chaud-froid sauce, decorated (mosaique style) with ox-tongue, truffles, French beans, carrots, etc., neatly dished in a border of Russian salad.

Oeufs a la Nantua.

Fried eggs, neatly trimmed, dished on a salpicon of shrimps or prawns, garnished with Nantua sauce.

Oeufs a la Niqoise.

Poached eggs, dished on rounds of duchesse puree, garnished with French beans and sauteed tomatoes.

Oeufs a l'Orleans.

Oval tartlet crusts three-parts filled with delicate brown chicken salpicon, with poached egg in each, sauced or coated with bechamel, and garnished with a round of pistachio border.

Oeufs a la Palestine.

Rounds or ovals of potato puree mixed with artichoke puree, ranged on dish, and each filled with raw egg, sauced over with a little cream, seasoned and carefully baked in oven.

Oeufs a la Perigueux.

Poached eggs, dressed in border of chicken puree (farce), and served with rich truffle sauce.

Oeufs a la Portugaise.

Sauteed tomatoes well blended with onions, fried in oil, ranged on a dish with neatly poached eggs on top.

Oeufs a la Poulette.

Moulded eggs (hard or soft-boiled), coated with supreme sauce, decorated and sprinkled with fine herbs.

Oeufs a la Princiere.

Croustades of bread or rice with poached egg in each, garnished with asparagus points; sauce Veloutee.

Oeufs a la Rachel.

Scrambled eggs mixed with strips of truffles and asparagus points.

Oeufs a la Reine Margot.

Scrambled eggs, dressed in croustades of puff pastry moistened with very little rich bechamel sauce.

Oeufs a la Romaine.

Fried eggs ranged on a bed of spinach sauteed whole (en branches), garnished with anchovy fillets, sprinkled with parmesan cheese, and slightly browned in the oven.

Oeufs a la Rossini.

Eggs fried on plates (sur plats), trimmed and placed on foie-gras puree, with a border of perigord sauce round each.

Oeufs a la Sevigne.

Poached eggs, placed on crusts of fried bread, coated with veloutee sauce, each decorated with a slice of truffle, and garnished with braised lettuce.

Oeufs a la Soubise.

Egg-shaped tartlet paste crusts, lined with soubise puree (onion), with poached egg on top.

Oeufs a la Turbigo.

Fried eggs, trimmed neatly, garnished with slices of sausages, fried ham, and tomatoes.

Oeufs a la Vatel.

Cassolette cases lined with a salpicon of sweetbread and scrambled eggs, mixed with shredded tomatoes and truffles.

Oeufs a la Verdi.

Poached eggs on fried bread croutes, coated over with sauce Venitienne, and decorated with truffle.

Oeufs a la Victoria.

Fried eggs, placed on lobster and truffle puree or salpicon, coated with lobster sauce.

Oeufs a la Yvette.

Scrambled eggs mixed with crayfish-tails, garnished with asparagus points, and served with sauce Venitienne.

Oeufs a la Zingara.

Poached eggs on oval-shaped croutons of fried bread, served with tomato and Madere sauces blended, and decorated with chopped ham.

Miscellaneous

Bouquet Garni

The bouquet garni is the mainstay of the French cuisine, and well it may be; it is more delicate and subtle than spices or dried condiments are apt to be. Usually the bouquet garni is composed of sprigs of chervil, chives, thyme, bay-leaves, tarragon, and parsley.

Nouille Paste (Pate Nouilles).

1 lb. flour,
1½ oz. butter,
2 small whole or 3 yolks of eggs,
a pinch of salt,
a little milk or water, if found necessary.

Sift the flour on to the pastry slab, make a well in the centre. Add the salt, eggs, and butter. Mix thoroughly and knead to a stiff but elastic paste; a little milk or water should be added with the eggs. Great care must, however, be taken not to make the paste too soft.

This paste requires at least fifteen minutes' kneading. Divide into pieces, roll out very thinly, and use as directed.

Salpicon.

A salpicon is a mince of either chicken, game, foie-gras or veal, with tongue, ham, mushrooms, and truffles.
The whole is cut into small dice and put into some prepared sauce — allemande, bechamel, or brown sauce. Salpicon is mostly used for filling bouchees (small puff-paste patties), when it is heated up in the sauce.
Oysters and lobsters, shrimps, and fillets of sole are frequently used for bouchees, in which case the filling is prepared as above, and is known under the general n.ame of Salpicon, ham or tongue being of course omitted.

Sauce Allemande (German Sauce).

1½ oz. butter,
1 oz. flour,
2 yolks of eggs,
1 tablespoonful of cream,
1 tea-spoonful lemon-juice,
chicken stock,
nutmeg,
salt,
pepper.

Melt the butter in a stewpan, add the flour, stir a few minutes without allowing it to brown, dilute with rather more than a pint of chicken stock, and stir until it boils. Season with pepper and salt and grated nutmeg. Let it simmer for half an hour, skim, and finish with a liaison made of the yolks of eggs, the cream, and ½ oz. of fresh butter. Stir over the fire until the eggs begin to set, but do not let it boil ; add the lemon-juice, and pass through a fine strainer or tammy cloth.

Sauce Anchois (Anchovy Sauce).

1 oz. butter,
¾ oz. flour,
½ pint milk,
¼ pint fish stock,
1 dessertspoonful anchovy essence.

Melt the butter in a stewpan, stir in the flour, mix well, and cook a little. Add by degrees the milk and the fish stock. Stir till it boils, and let cook for lo minutes. Incorporate a small dessertspoonful of anchovy essence, boil up again and strain.

Sauce Aurora.

½ pint of bechamel sauce,
2 oz. butter,
1 oz. lobster butter,
½ gill cream,
1 dessertspoonful tarragon vinegar,
cayenne.

Put the bechamel sauce in a stewpan, add the butter, a pinch of cayenne, cream, tarragon vinegar, and lobster butter. Stir well over boiling water till hot, but without letting the sauce boil.

Sauce Bechamel.

1½ oz. flour,
2 oz. butter,
1¼ pint of milk,
and white meat stock,
1 small onion or shallot,
1 small bouquet garni,
10 peppercorns,
½ a bay-leaf,

1 small blade of mace,
seasoning.

Put the milk on to boil with the onion or shallot (peeled), the bouquet, peppercorns, mace, and bay-leaf. Melt the butter, stir in the flour, and cook a little without browning (or use white roux), stir in the milk, etc. (hot), whisk over the fire until it boils, and let simmer from fifteen to twenty minutes. Take out the bouquet, rub through a sieve or tammy, return to the stewpan, season lightly with a pinch of nutmeg, half-pinch of cayenne, and half a teaspoonful of salt. The sauce is then ready for use.

Sauce Bordeaux.

Peel and mince finely two shallots, reduce with 1 gill of claret with ½ a teaspoonful of crushed white peppercorns, a sprig of thyme, and a sprig of marjoram. When about half reduced, add 1 gill of espagnole sauce, and boil for 10 minutes, then strain, re-heat, and whisk in i teaspoonful of anchovy or crayfish butter. Season to taste, and use as directed.

Sauce Bearnaise.

½ gill tarragon vinegar,
3 shallots finely chopped,
6 peppercorns, cruslied,
4 yolks of eggs,
1 tablespoonful of white sauce,
4 oz. butter,
1 sprig thyme,
meat glaze,
lemon-juice.

Put the shallots, peppercorns, and thyme with the vinegar in a stewpan, cover and boil until well reduced, remove the thyme, add the sauce and a little dissolved meat glaze. Wisk in the yolks of eggs, taking care not to let the sauce boil, remove the stewpan from the fire, and work in by degrees the butter. Only a little butter must be added at a time, otherwise the sauce will get oily. Strain through a pointed strainer or tammy. A little finely chopped fresh tarragon and chervil, and a few drops of lemon-juice may be added after the sauce is strained.

Sauce Bordelaise (Claret Sauce).

¾ pint espagnole sauce, or brown sauce,
1 wineglassful claret,
2 finely chopped shallots,
½ oz. meat glaze,
1 teaspoonful chopped herbs (parsley, tarragon, and chervil),
a pinch of sugar,
salt and pepper.

Put the wine and shallots in a stewpan, reduce to half, add the sauce, and cook slowly for twenty minutes. Take off the scum, add the chopped herbs and meat glaze. Season with sugar, salt, and pepper. Give it one more boil, and keep hot in the bain-marie until required.

Note . — In most cases where bordelaise sauce is used, and especially so with beef, some thin round slices of beef marrow are blanched and put on the meat before it is served, or else warmed up in the sauce.

Brown Fish Sauce (Sauce Brune, Brown Sauce).

½ lb. fish-bones, etc.,
1½ oz. butter,
1 dessertspoonful of flour,
1 tablespoonful Brown & Poison's patent cornflour,
1 gill claret (optional),
¾ pint fish stock or water,
1 sliced onion,

1 small bunch savoury herbs (bouquet garni),
4 mushrooms,
salt and pepper to taste.

Fry the fish-bones, etc., in the butter over a quick fire, add the onion and fry also, stir in the flour and cornflour, and let the flour get brown whilst stirring ; add the carrot, herbs, and mushrooms, and moisten with the claret and the stock. Stir till it boils and let simmer for twenty minutes. Pass through a tammy cloth or fine sieve, season to taste, and serve. If liked the mushrooms may be chopped finely and put into the sauce at the last.

Sauce Cardinal.

½ pint veloutee or bechamel sauce,
1 oz. butter,
juice of ½ lemon,
½ oz. lobster coral or 1 oz. lobster butter,
1 dessertspoonful meat glaze,
½ gill mushroom liquor,
salt,
pepper,
nutmeg.

Reduce the sauce with the mushroom liquor, season with salt, pepper, and a grate of nutmeg; add the lemon-juice, and whisk in the butter and lobster butter or coral, the latter finely chopped. Strain or tammy. Return to the stewpan and add the meat glaze, stir till smooth, and keep hot in the bain-marie till required.

Sauce Chaud-froid, blanche (White Chaud-froid Sauce).

½ pint bechamel or supreme sauce,
1 gill aspic,
5 or 6 leaves gelatine.

1 gill cream,
1 teaspoonful chilli vinegar or lemon-juice.

Dissolve the gelatine along with the aspic jelly, warm up the sauce, and mix the two together. Stir over the fire imtil it boils, put in vinegar or lemon-juice, and cook for a few minutes. Strain or tammy; add the cream when cooling, and use as required.

Sauce Colbert aux Fines Herbes (Brown Herb Sauce).

½ gill espagnole sauce,
1 glass or Madeira wine,
1 tablespoonful of meat glaze,
1½ oz. of fresh butter,
1 teaspoonful lemon juice,
chopped parsley,
tarragon, and chervil — one dessertspoonful in all.

Put the sauce into a small stewpan, stir over the fire until hot, add the wine, and let boil a few minutes. Remove to the side of the stove, and stir in gradually the butter and the meat glaze. Beat up with a small whisk, but do not let it boil again. Last of all add the lemon juice and the chopped herbs. Serve as directed. If desired richer, ½ oz. more butter may be added in the manner described.

Curry Sauce. (See "Sauce Indienne")

Sauce Demi-Glace (Half-Glaze Sauce).

¾ pint espagnole sauce,
1½ gill good gravy,
pepper.

Reduce (half-glaze) espagnole sauce (see below), with the gravy (strained and free from fat) ; allow to simmer about fifteen minutes, and season with a pinch of pepper.

Sauce Espagnole (Spanish Sauce).

3 quarts of rich stock,
4 oz. lean veal,
1 bouquet garni,
12 peppercorns,
4 oz. butter,
4 oz. flour (sifted),
4 oz. raw ham or lean bacon,
1 carrot,
1 onion,
2 cloves,
½ pint tomato pulp,
1 gill claret, i glass sherry, some mushrooms (fresh or preserved).

This is the chief brown foundation sauce — it forms the basis for a large number of other sauces. It is advisable that particular care and attention be paid to the preparation of this important sauce. The ingredients given will produce about half a gallon of sauce. A smaller quantity can be prepared by reducing the quantities in proportion. It is, however, advisable to have at all times an ample supply of this sauce.
Wash and peel the carrot, turnip, and onion, cut up small and put in a stewpan with the bouquet, peppercorns, cloves, and the veal and ham, both cut into pieces. Add an ounce of butter, and stir over the fire until of a nice light brown colour; this forms a true mirepoix. Pour off the fat, moisten the mirepoix with the stock, claret, sherry, and tomato pulp, boil gently for about an hour. Skim occasionally. Meanwhile, prepare a brown roux by melting 3 oz. of butter in a stewpan, stir in the flour, and cook very slowly over a moderate fire, stirring all the while with a wooden spoon until it acquires a chestnut-brown colour; or place the stewpan in the oven and let it

cook, stirring from time to time to prevent it from burning, and to blend the flour better. Allow the roux to cool a little, pour in gradually the prepared stock, etc., stir over the fire until it boils, let simmer slowly for another hour, skim well, and pass through a tammy cloth or fine sieve. If found too thick, add a little more stock. To prevent a thick crust forming on the top of the sauce, stir occasionally until quite cool. Keep the sauce in a stone vessel or pan until wanted. Be sure and boil up the sauce each day if not used up at one time, adding a little stock if necessary.

Sauce Homard (Lobster Sauce).

Take half a pint of bechamel, add to it two heaped-up tablespoonfuls of finely chopped lobster, including a little coral or spawn; mix, and heat up carefully whilst stirring; season with a pinch of cayenne or paprika pepper, and serve when hot.

Sauce Indienne (Indian Curry Sauce).

1½ oz. butter,
½ oz. flour,
½ small onion,
1 tablespoonful curry-powder,
¾ pint good stock,
salt,
1 tomato,
a few savoury herbs,
½ glass sherry or Marsala.

Melt the butter, add the onion, finely chopped; when of a nice light brown stir in the flour and curry-powder, blend well, and cook for five minutes; pour in gradually the stock, add the tomato, cut into slices, and the herbs; bring it to the boil whilst stirring, then add the wine, season to taste, cook for twenty minutes, then strain and serve.

Sauce Italienne (Italian Sauce).

½ pint espagnole sauce,
4 small shallots,
8 preserved mushrooms,
a sprig of thyme,
1 bay-leaf,
1 tablespoonful sweet oil,
1 glass Chablis or Sauterne,
½ gill stock.

Peel the shallots, chop them finely, place in the corner of a clean cloth, hold tightly wrapped up under cold water, then squeeze out the water, and put them in a small stewpan with the oil, stir over the fire for a few minutes, to blend but not to colour. Add the wine, the mushrooms (finely chopped), herbs, and the stock, let it reduce well, and add the espagnole. Boil for ten minutes, take out the herbs, free it from the oil, and keep hot in the bain-marie until required.

Sauce Madere (Madeira Sauce).

Proceed the same as directed for Demi-glace sauce. Add one glass of sherry or Marsala; reduce a little longer, then add a little meat glaze to give it additional richness.

Sauce Mornay.

½ pint bechamel sauce,
½ gill mushroom or Italienne sauce,
½ gill cream,
½ oz. meat glaze or 2 tablespoonfuls half-glaze of chicken stock,
1 oz. grated Parmesan cheese,
1 oz. fresh butter.

Put the bechamel sauce into a saucepan, reduce it well, then add the Italian or mushroom sauce. Let it boil up, skim well, and add the cream. Place the stewpan in a vessel of boiling water, stir the sauce with a whisk, adding the grated cheese, butter, and meat glaze; work in these ingredients little by little, and stir or whisk till the sauce has acquired a creamy texture. Do not allow the sauce to boil again. This sauce is usually served with fish — in which case a little fish essence should also be incorporated before serving.

Sauce Mousseline Verte (Green Mousseline Sauce, cold).

1 gill mayonnaise,
½ gill cold bechamel sauce,
1 tablespoonful of pickled parsley,
a few sprigs each of tarragon, chervil, and burnet,
2 tablespoonfuls of cooked spinach,
2 hard-boiled yolks of eggs,
2 anchovy fillets,
½ gill of cream.

Wash and pick the green herbs, steep them in boiling water for a few minutes, drain well, pound in a mortar with the spinach, and rub through a fine sieve. Pound the yolks of eggs and anchovy fillets, mix with the green puree, add the cream, and rub the whole through a sieve. Dilute with mayonnaise and bechamel sauce, add a little seasoning and a teaspoonful of mixed mustard.

Melted Butter Sauce (Sauce Anglaise).

1 oz. fresh butter,
¾ oz. Hour,
½ pint cold water.

Put the butter in a saucepan, when melted stir in the flour (sifted). Cook for a few moments whilst stirring, add gradually ½ pint of cold water, continue to stir till the sauce boils, and allow to cook for at least ten minutes. Add salt and pepper to taste, and strain if necessary.

Sauce Nantua.

Bechamel reduced with fish essence and finished with crayfish butter.

Onion Sauce (Sauce aux Oignons).

2 onions,
1 oz. butter,
½ oz. flour,
½ pint milk,
nutmeg.

Peel the onions, cut them in halves and blanch them, drain and cook them in salted water till tender, drain again and chop finely. Melt the butter in a saucepan, stir in the flour, cook a little and add gradually the milk; stir till it boils and put in the chopped onions, season with pepper and a grate of nutmeg, and cook for ten minutes longer.

Note. — When Brown onion sauce is required, mince the onions and fry a light brown colour in butter, drain off the butter and add half a pint of brown sauce, cook for fifteen minutes

Sauce Perigueux (Truffle Sauce, Perigord Sauce).

1 gill brown sauce,
1 gill tomato sauce,
1 glass sherry,
1 teaspoonful anchovy sauce,

1 oz. butter,
3 truffles.

Chop finely three large truffles, put them in a small stewpan with the sherry, reduce to one-half (covered) ; add the brown and tomato sauce p. i6o) ; boil for a few minutes, finish with a teaspoonful of anchovy essence and the butter.

Sauce Piquante (Sharp Sauce).

½ onion or 4 shallots,
3 gherkins (chopped),
1 tablespoonful chopped capers,
I gill vinegar,
½ teaspoonful anchovy essence,
1 bay-leaf,
1 sprig of thyme,
¾ pint espagnole sauce.

Peel and chop the onion or shallots, put them in a stewpan with the vinegar, bay-leaf, and thyme, cover, and reduce to half the quantity of liquor. Strain into another stewpan, add the chopped gherkins and capers, moisten with the sauce, add the anchovy essence, boil a few minutes, and serve.

Sauce Poivrade (Pepper Satice).

¾ pint of espagnole sauce,
½ oz. of butter,
½ small carrot,
½ small onion,
18 peppercorns,
1 bay-leaf,
1 sprig thyme, 2 cloves,
½ oz. of raw ham or bacon.

Mince the onion and carrot, cut the ham or bacon into small pieces; fry the above in the butter for three minutes, add the peppercorns (crushed), herbs, etc. ; skim off the fat, moisten with the sauce, and boil for ten minutes or longer ; skim, strain, and serve as required.

Sauce Remoulade.

½ pint salad oil,
2 tablespoonfuls tarragon vinegar,
1 teaspoonful made mustard,
tarragon,
parsley,
burnet,
chives,
1 yolk of egg,
castor sugar.

Blanch a few leaves of tarragon, parsley, burnet, and chives, drain and chop finely. Put in a basin the yolk of egg with salt and pepper to taste, stir well with a wooden spoon, work in gradually half a pint of salad oil, and at intervals a few drops of tarragon vinegar. About two tablespoonfuls of vinegar is required to half a pint of oil. When the sauce is finished add a teaspoonful of made mustard, a pinch of castor sugar, and the chopped herbs,

Sauce Supreme.

1 oz. butter,
1 oz. flour,
1 pint chicken stock,
1 small onion,
1 clove,
½ bay- leaf,
3 oz. fresh butter,
1 tablespoonful cream,
1 yolk of egg,

½ lemon.

Make a white roux with the butter and flour, and dilute with the chicken stock. Boil up, add the onion, clove, half bay-leaf, and let it simmer for fifteen minutes. Skim well, and work in the butter, cream, yolk of egg, and the juice of half a lemon. Whisk well, and pass through a tammy cloth.

Sauce Tomate (Tomato Sauce).

1½ pint stock,
1 oz. streaky bacon,
1 oz. butter,
1 small onion finely chopped,
1 lb. tomatoes,
1 oz. flour,
peppercorns,
herbs,
parsley,
1 oz. fresh butter,
castor sugar.

Put into a stewpan the butter and onion, fry a little, and add the tomatoes cut into slices. Stir over the fire a little longer, then add the flour previously mixed with a little cold stock or gravy. Stir the stock in gradually, add a few peppercorns, a few sprigs of savoury herbs and parsley, and allow all to simmer for half an our. Remove the herbs, rub the sauce through a sieve, return to the stewpan, season with salt, a pinch of castor sugar and pepper, whisk the butter, and serve as required. A tablespoonful of cream can be used instead of butter, but the sauce should not be allowed to boil again after the butter or cream has been added.

Sauce Venitienne.

½ pint allemande or bechamel sauce,
1 oz. lobster butter,
1 dessertspoonful meat glaze,

the juice of half a lemon, pepper,
nutmeg,
salt,
1 teaspoonful finely chopped tarragon leaves.

Heat up the sauce, stir in the lobster butter and meat glaze when required for serving, add lemon-juice, sufficient pepper, grated nutmeg, and salt to taste, and, last of all, the chopped tarragon.

Sauce Veloutee (Velvet Sauce).

1 oz. flour,
½ t oz. butter,
1 pint of veal stock,
¼ gill mushroom liquor,
½ gill of cream,
1 small bouquet garni,
6 peppercorns,
salt,
nutmeg,
lemon juice.

Cook the flour and i oz. of butter together without browning, stir in the stock and mushroom liquor, add the bouquet and crushed peppercorns, boil slowly for twenty minutes, stir frequently, and skim. Pass through a sieve or tammy; keep on the side of the stove, put a few tiny pieces of butter on top to keep from forming a skin. Just before using it add the cream. Stir well and let it get thoroughly hot without boiling, season with salt if necessary, a pinch of nutmeg, and about a teaspoonful of lemon-juice. The sauce is now ready for use, and will serve as a foundation for any white sauce or as a veloutee by itself. The cream may be omitted if used as a foundation sauce.

Simple White Sauce.

1 oz. butter,
1 oz. flour,
½ pint milk,
½ gill white stock or water,
½ bay-leaf,
salt and white pepper.

Melt the butter in a small, saucepan, stir in the flour, and cook for a few minutes without allowing the flour to brown; dilute with the milk, stir till it boils, then add the stock and bay-leaf, and let simmer for at least ten minutes. Remove the bay-leaf, season to taste, and strain.

Sauce Chivry

An allemande sauce with blanched and chopped herbs: tarragon, spinach, parsley and or chervil

Sauce Choron.

Bearnaise sauce blended with tomato puree.

Sauce a la Creme (Cream Sauce).

Bechamel or supreme sauce finished with fresh cream as liaison.

Sauce Paprika.

Veloutee or allemande sauce highly seasoned with paprika or red Hungarian pepper.

Printed in Great Britain
by Amazon